Rules

by Barbara L. Luciano

PEARSON

Scott
Foresman

Editorial Offices: Glenview, Illinois • Parsippany, New Jersey • New York, New York
Sales Offices: Needham, Massachusetts • Duluth, Georgia • Glenview, Illinois
Coppell, Texas • Sacramento, California • Mesa, Arizona

We follow rules.

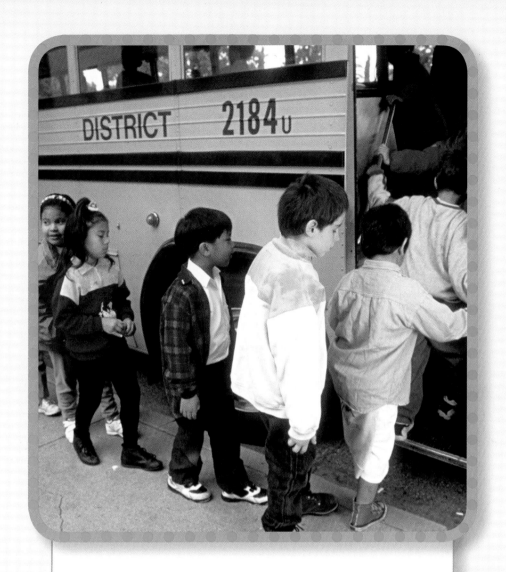

We line up for the bus.

We share our books.

We help at home.

We listen at school.

What are your rules?

Glossary

help to do a job or chore

listen to pay attention to someone's words

share to take turns using something